Metamorphosis
Changes of the Heart

Andrea Erickson

Illustrations by Judith Gosse

To order additional copies of this book, contact:
Xlibris
844-714-8691
www.Xlibris.com
Orders@Xlibris.com

ISBN: Softcover   979-8-3694-0446-1
       EBook   979-8-3694-0445-4

Print information available on the last page

Rev. date: 07/31/2023

Contents

An Introduction vii

Awakening..1

Excuse me 2

Tastes of you 3

Oz...4

Cowboy..5

DJ 6

Heartstrings 7

Quasimodo 8

Tasting the universe 9

Steel perfection..10

Courage 12

Growth 13

Number 2 14

Boardwalk 15

Crossroads and Questions 16

Airport Diner 17

The Haunting...18

Crossroad 19

Holiday 20

The Affair 21

Time 22

The smell of Thanksgiving 23

Creation 24

Struggle **26**

Maybe tomorrow 27

Grief 28

Little Monsters 30

Lost Love 31

Jaynie 32

Rupture 35

No rain 36

Tarnished Wings 37

Indifference 38

The Christmas Tree 39

Rebirth **40**

The Watchdog from Pompeii 41

High Flight 42

Peace 43

Calm after the Storm 44

Extraordinary day 45

Independence 46

Fall in New England 47

Midnight 48

I give thanks 49

Becoming 50

Dedicated to those who changed me, and the man who won my heart.

An Introduction

Our lives are in a constant state of change from the moment we take our first breath, to the moment we depart. This includes our growing self-awareness, our families and friends, and our partners: each play profound roles in shaping our identity and our understanding of the world. "Metamorphosis" is a collection of poems that explore the complex landscape of the transformations we experience throughout our lives. Like the weather, our relationships are often subject to the ebbs and flows of life, and this collection captures the essence of those moments.

The first section, "The Awakening" takes us on a voyage of discovery, as our souls begin to explore the depths of our physical, emotional, and spiritual connections to ourselves and each other. These poems capture the excitement and enchantment of new love; the fear of rejection and living on our own; the thrill of expectation and revelation; and the growth that comes from these distinct emotions.

"Growth" delves deeper into the heart of relationships, exploring the vulnerability and trust required to forge strong bonds. Through these poems, we uncover the beauty of true connection, as well as the challenges that arise as we surrender ourselves to each other. This section speaks to the profound courage and strength that is necessary for lasting love within our lives.

As with all things in life, relationships are not without their challenges. In "Struggle," we confront the obstacles and trials that test the strength of our love. These poems expose the raw emotions of heartache, conflict, and self-doubt as we navigate the tempestuous seas of human connection. Yet, in these moments of adversity, we also find the potential for understanding, and renewal.

Finally, "Rebirth" takes us to a place of transformation, as we emerge from the ashes of our past experiences, ready to embrace a new chapter in our lives. These poems celebrate the resilience of the human spirit, as we forge new paths, rediscover spiritual plateaus, and cultivate a deep appreciation for the power of love.

In "Metamorphosis," you will find a mirror reflecting the beauty and complexity of ourselves and each other. Through these poems, you are invited to examine your own journey, to uncover the many paths that have shaped your life, guide you through the ever-changing perspective of love, connection, and self-discovery and to celebrate your own metamorphosis.

Awakening

Excuse me

Excuse me,
But, your love is showing.

Tastes of you

I Dine
On candle light and wine,
I Feast
on fantasies and passion;
for these are the morsels left
to Savor
when the full moon's light
breaks through evening's veil,
to Touch
and illuminate your memory.

Oz

Here.
In the land of Oz,
we stand and wait
searching for answers
that appear on the crystal ball…
The Wizard
cannot answer our questions.
He is too busy with his games
of illusion
and
delusion.
What shall we do?
The balloon will be flying soon -
the North wind is ready
to carry it away
over rainbows
and
clouds,
while we remain in Oz,
waiting for the crystal ball
and the answers…

Cowboy

He sits astride his horse
Beyond the arching mountain range,
in a valley of pinecones and snow,
where nothing touches him
but time, space, and other Lovers.
I've heard some call him Cowboy –
A rock 'n' roll wizard
Wheeling passion and power.
He plays the game with style and grace,
Twirling his rope of fantasies
high in the air,
like an old-time western hero
who rode the range in a long ago dream.
They say he loves the rodeo,
and cowboy boots,
and ladies,
and riding high above the crowds
on his horse of Silver-gray.
sometimes at night I think of him,
and his Green-Eyed Gaze that captured me,
and I wonder if he ever tires
of life inside a Fantasy.

DJ

He sits behind the airwaves.
A man of many moods.
He cuts and tapes his days away,
to the sound of forties tunes.
His eyes are painted tired,
the lighting strains his view;
but, the tune in the end has
a powerful pull –
the choices, if any, are few.
But, the beat goes on in silence,
while the rat race hums along.
The drifters make their way back home.
Ain't that how it goes in song?

So, he mingles with the madness
from lowlife to insane;
from exhaustion to perfection –
is life the one to blame?
I watched him sleeping late last night.
His hands were lax and still,
his face was like a child's at rest.
The night, reprieve from will.
But, the beat thumps on in silence,
while the rat race hums along.
The drifters make their way back home.
Ain't that how it goes in song?

Heartstrings

We tug at each other's Heartstrings.
Two children at play.
Innocent offenders rolling down dangerous slopes,
stubbornly accepting Fate as the final judge and jury.
Truth
or Consequences.
they are one-in-the-same in our Game.
Yet, we talk each other
tender
until it Hurts.

Quasimodo

Notre Dame stands tall, now that Quasimodo fell;
the hands that gripped the stone-faced men
have shriveled up in hell.
He lived his life in solitude –
a victim of God's will.
the spires of the church's grace –
his world's own windowsill.
A folly of a man they said - an imbecile, a freak.
But, he saved the honor of his love, though he could not hear or speak.
I met him in a dream one night,
in the darkest dark of the morning's light
and his face was grieved, but his eyes shone bright –
for he'd tasted Love through distorted life.
The good die young, so it says in song.
So, tell me why, my friend,
do sincere at heart never play the part
of winner in the end.

Tasting the universe

I would like to hold a piece of Heaven.
just for a while…
I would like to hold the stars and galaxies within my hands.
I'd like to see them grow and die,
only to be created again.

I'd like to smell eternity
just for a while…
I'd like to hear a falling star
break the limits of space and time.

I'd like to taste the universe,
Savor the juices in my mouth.
just for a while.

Steel perfection

I'm human. Is that a sin?
I show signs of emotion; the rope to do
you in.
I awaken in the morning
and send you all my love.
I buy you books and building blocks
and green-eyed turtle doves.
But, you?
your sheer perfection –
From toenail to gold molar.
a god in flesh – you outshine light –
you're always right
a shooting star…
So, try a Robot Outlet – full of steel
perfection,
just hug those metal marvels –

they're the mothers of invention.

I'm sure you'll find your size:

right shape, right shade, right form.

Like you, my dear, I'm sure you'll find,

they're far beyond the norm.

Not me – I'm flesh and blood.

I work a job, I drink too much, I've even played in mud.

But, soil-free is your taste -

close ties will do you in.

No way to shoot for less than ten.

You have to be the best to win.

So, try a Robot Outlet – full of steel perfection.

Courage

Paths are just taken,
leading us to byways
that seem peaceful and welcome.
We cannot foresee the storms
that may steer us to dangerous places.
And neither can we know if we will survive.
Our strength lies in our courage
to continue walking,
hoping,
and
praying
that the rainbow does have an end.
and
Oz is a place in the sun.

Growth

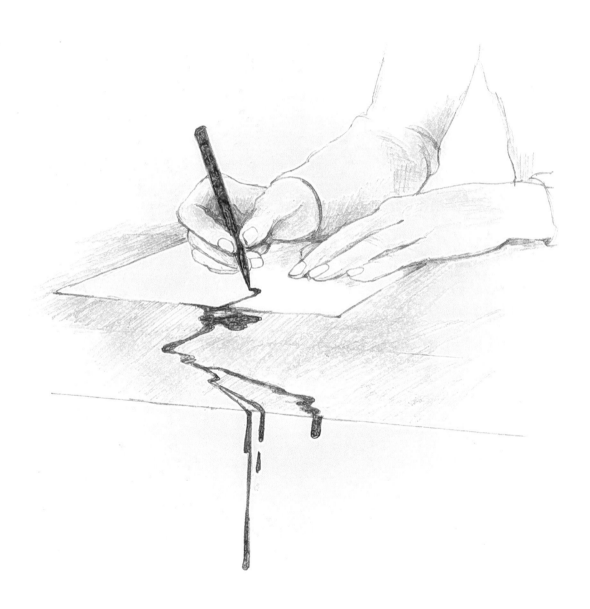

Number 2

I crushed you beneath my pen
and scrawled your blood
across the neat blue and white bleeding sheets
you tried to crawl away
to slip and slide from the pages
but I caught you with my penpoint,
pressed you back to the white
and watched your heart
tear
and bleed
as you have watched mine
so many times before.

Boardwalk

The boardwalk squeaks loudly
this dismal evening
recalling the sun
and laughter of the season.

But, I walk alone
A specter in the night
tasting of stale beer –
reminiscing on his light.

A tear falls silently
from my cheek
disappearing onto dried wood.
I can hear distant laughter…
How I wish I could.

Far out on the open sea
A ship sails alone.
Oh, how I pray
that it's travelling home.

Crossroads and Questions

The trials we endure in our growing,
keep pulling our childhoods apart.
The years that we waste always wishing
for someone to comfort our hearts,
lead us to crossroads and questions
and stages of life so unknown
that nightmares are pleasant to deal with,
and daylight sheds no sight of home.

Airport Diner

Voices bounce against each other and echo
against thick, glass restaurant walls.
The heavy sound of dishes clashing against one another
shout out from the kitchen door.
Silverware and glassware chime in,
while the abbreviated sentences of diners
add to the breakfast noise - a conflagration of sounds.

The airport diner.
A stop for waves of hungry wayfarers waiting for their turn
to eat and run.
Waiting for their turn to consume words, meals and time before they fly away,
Leaving echoes of chatter in their wake.

The Haunting

She watches in melancholy madness,
working on green and on gray;
while counting the ants on her doorstep,
she cries all the warm nights away.

Her eyes are distorted and tired,
red, swollen, and sore.
Her shoulders are burdened from pressures.
Her mind always thinking of yore.

Why do we waste all the sunshine,
when storms are so fierce and so gray?
When rains wash away all our daydreams,
and mornings are lightyears away?

I long for the laughter of children
free and unhampered by pain;
but, waking to music each morning,
I'm greeted by darkness and rain.

Crossroad

Slipping into the black night to find myself, again.
No uniform.
No rules.
No mask.
Just me and the knowledge that I'm standing naked
at a new beginning.
There is no crossroad here.
Just open highway and the dreams I left along the way,
to grab the golden ring.

Holiday

May you find
the Light in the eyes of a child,
a Path when none can be seen,
Magic in the mundane,
Laughter to ease a pain,
Love in the heart of a stranger,
Joy in the notes of a song,
and Hope in tomorrow's dawn.

The Affair

He deals in large numbers;
I study the stars,
he invests all his money,
while I analyze Mars,
He reads Wall Street Journal;
I write poetry,
He's committed to marriage,
as I wander free.
Hair tinted with silver –
mine, blonde from the sun,
His life is determined,
while I've just begun.
He lives in the mountains,
the ocean's my home.
His family surrounds him –
I'm out on my own.

So, what have we gained
in our quest for a dream?
Two opposites living
a life that's unseen.
We share sheltered moments
in dark and in pine.
We live day-to-day
and drink pricey wine.
We touch in our daydreams,
we love through the wires,
our whispers reveal
that in passion, there's fire.
But, tomorrow is never –
our time is on hold.
No joy-ever-after.
The story's been told.

Time

Slow down Father time.
Rest a while.
Lay your sickle
beneath the weeping willow
and sleep.
Let your sons rest their weary arms.
Let them unwind.
Take them away
from the ticking and talking
and ringing.
Find your Grand Father.
Remove him from his corner
and stop his pendulum.
Let him feel the peace and serenity
of Death.
Slow down Father Time.
And live.

The smell of Thanksgiving

The smell of Thanksgiving crept into my bedroom at sunrise – turkey, stuffing, onions, squash… The sound of hushed voices from my parents joined the scent, as I curled up under the blanket like a contented kitten expecting the day to be as welcoming as the scent of the morning that teased me.

The touch of the satin edge of my blanket rubbing softly between my thumb and fingers, provided a satisfying interlude while I waited for life to awaken in other rooms before I rolled out of bed. The warm rays of daylight filtering through the curtains confirmed that the day had indeed begun.

It's been so long since the scent of Thanksgiving greeted me that way. It's hard to believe it ever happened at times.
The cuddled up moments awaiting the taste of turkey skin with dressing, apple pie, and chocolate cream…
My brother and I playing games with our cousins
while we sipped ginger ale and orange soda.

So long ago. Or, was it yesterday?
My mother has been dead for a long time.
I have been separated from my husband for a long time too.
I wonder if this is the end of the smell of Thanksgiving,
or if other mornings – yet undiscovered – will carry its scent to my bedroom,
and again let me curl up under the blanket like a contented kitten.

Creation

I scrambled.
Searching for my muse.
The muse of inviting kisses.
The muse of warm embraces.
The muse of lust.
The muse of passion.
I could not find her.
Yet, she was here.
Somewhere.
Hidden between pages, and memories.
Hidden above sawdust on old shelves.
Hidden in childhood dreams.
Yet, she vanished.
Without cause.
Without warning.
Without reason.
No muse?
No verse.
No rhyme.

Silence.

All was quiet.

Then, suddenly there was a sound.

A quiet sound.

A flutter.

A whisper.

Slowly, flowers bloomed in far off halls.

Memories fell from the ceiling.

Dust flew from aged photos.

And, I started to see,

My Muse was within me.

I could see her grace.

Her wonder.

Love notes flew from her fingertips.

Harmonies, and melodies echoed in the air around her.

Faces of poets and balladeers shown above her

Like translucent shadows in the light.

And then, I wrote…

Struggle

Maybe tomorrow

Constellations
march across the sky.
I stare.
Stars wink back from Heaven.
Cool August nights roll in
from the sea.
A blanket of wonder surrounds me.
Alone.
It's different now.
Crickets chirp along the riverside,
while water laps
against the shore in time to the beats.
I want to find the meaning of it all.
Maybe someday.
Maybe tomorrow.

Grief

It's something intangible.
Yet, it has substance.
Yet, it can't be defined - this hole in my soul.
It is a hole, but it has structure like a great darkness sitting in my gut.
There are more holes. Big holes that didn't exist when you lived.
Why now? This is a question I can't answer.
No one can.
I cry at times when I know no one is looking.
You were so large.
You were the laughter in the room.
The smiles that painted every face.
The hammers that hit every nail.

The boots that trekked through mud.

The songs.

The bass note.

The trombone slide.

The harmonies.

But, no.

There are so many holes.

Holes that cannot be filled without you.

My Dad.

Why didn't you wait for me?

Maybe my soul would not feel so abandoned.

Maybe the gaps of who you were would fill in the empty spaces.

Make me feel complete.

There remains a hole in my soul without you.

Little Monsters

I found light in your departure.
Another side of a complicated bleeder.
Capable of more than her unique little monster believed.
Were these the beasts that found each other?
Did we come along for the ride?
Is it possible they loved?
Not for a lifetime -
For moments…
So they could find peace?
The strangers in each of us found each other.
How sad to think we never did.

Lost Love

Monosyllables
drip
from
your
lips
like
drops
from
an
old
pipe.
One-
by-
one
they
fall
with
no
change
in
form
or
tone.

Jaynie

She was my dog.
I didn't choose her. She chose me.
And I loved her.
Deep within my heart and soul, I loved her.
She had the silkiest flat, dark coat.
She had a tiny scar on her nose.
She had a tail that stood up with wagging excitement and expectations.
She was kind to little girls.
She was kind to the vet.
She loved her parents, her sister, her aunts, and her cousins.
She loved her grandmother who fed her tasty morsels that I wouldn't.
She loved popcorn.
She was my dog.
Complete with imperfections and grace.
She was a rescue whose undistinguished lineage was royal to me.
I called her Jaynie, Janice Marie and Jane Jane.
She was a tiny dog with a tender heart and a fierce bark to protect me and announce her power.

She followed me. Everywhere. No leash required, just my voice.

She sat next to me in wide spaces.

She sat next to me in narrow spaces.

She wanted to be near.

She did not like to swim in water.

She did not like arms around her.

Except for Becca, who touched her canine spirit with safety and wonder.

She was my dog.

She loved to jump, hopping up as if her tiny legs were made of springs.

She loved her treats, she loved her turkey, cherry tomatoes and classical music.

She loved a road trip, laying her little body under my legs, and loving the new smells that tickled her nose.

She loved an adventure.

Except for the beach, where the sun and the heat were too bright.

She loved her couch, her silk pillow and her hiya hiya – her soft blanket that set her dreams in motion.

She loved her yard, running a lap around the pool each day with her little legs for exercise and to sniff out a bug or
two she encountered along the way.

She loved drinking old rain water from a small birdbath at her height.

She was my dog.

Barking excited greetings when I returned home,

Play jumping her joy, when she knew I would stay.

She was my dog.

She was my spitfire.

She was my baby.

I watched her grow for 15 years.

I protected her.

I was amazed by her.

I had to let her go when old age and sickness won the race.

She was my dog.

She loved me.

I loved her.

And I will miss her forever.

Rupture

You were part of a picture that I wanted us to live.

Cozy house nestled along a sidewalked street, light pouring from its windows during the early darkness of winter.

I wanted us to be a couple living in the cozy house, talking about our day, listening to the kids play games upstairs, the scent of roast chicken drifting out from the kitchen, feeling the warmth of the slow burning fire in the hearth, talking about our weekend plans and next vacation, while listening to the soft vibe of the latest jazz record you found in the store last week.

That's what I wanted.

Yet, there were no children, no early evening moments of conversation minus the TV, no evenings that brought us together before bedtime. I caught a disease that peels my strength away over time, you never wanted a child, I worked late at the office to support the household, and the home we finally owned together was our undoing.

And, yet; even still, while watching 'us' fall away from being one under God, I find a new layer of pain I didn't know I had anymore.

But it creeps up on me without warning,

And I stop.

And think about the house, light pouring from its windows in the early darkness of winter.

No rain

The rain will fall this weekend
and pool into buckets of water that invite warnings from weather forecasters.

Another transition in a very transitional year.

I miss you in many moments of my life now.
It makes me sad to think that I'm caught between not being able to live with you
And
not being able to live without you.
'Living with' is the operative phrase.
I can't do that with you.
We brought out the best and worst in each other.
And the best is hard to erase from all the years of learning to try and live with
the worst.

But the rain will still fall tomorrow and tomorrow.
And I'll be thinking of you in many moments of both.

You still flood my soul.

Tarnished Wings

I've turned this decision over
Five, ten, 15 billion times,
and still come back to the same question -
marking the ways in which this seems so right,
and so wrong.
How could I leave a man so brilliant, so handsome, so loving,
So wrong.
For me?
And then to ask myself, why?
No answer returning.
More questions.
Could this be a peri-menopausal shift in clarity,
Or something more subtle?
I don't know anymore.
I said I could never love another as deeply as I love you.
A truth that remains.
Did we have so much, or nothing at all?
The beautiful one has tarnished wings
You didn't see.

Indifference

I fear the indifference of men.
Of friends.
Of myself.
I wonder what it is.
that keeps me going.
That keeps me from falling apart?
The sandmen are all gone.
There's nothing left but me, myself and I -
and, sometimes
even we get lonely
for the fairytales,
and once-upon-a-time,
and the knights
in shining
armor.

The Christmas Tree

The tree went up last night.

Pre-lit and packaged like a pop-up candle.

It fit perfectly into the window.

No trimming needed, just decorations from days past.

But there was something missing.

The scent of pine and prickly needles that fell with their sappy mess onto the living room rug.

The scissors used to sculpt boughs, in hopes that gaps would disappear once limbs were illuminated.

The Christmas tree light test which revealed those that failed to survive to another Season.

The music of Johnny Mathis singing Ave Maria while I tenderly unwrapped my personal memories with each Christmas decoration.

And, I miss the 'big unveil' when complete.

Another memory.

Another life.

Rebirth

The Watchdog from Pompeii

I saw your body cast today.
The image of your twisted body -
your agony festered in my soul.
You must have struggled to escape from the heavy chain that bound you.
You must have crawled over the hills of acid dust growing around you.
Dust that scorched your brown eyes;
filled your lungs with sulfur;
dust that finally buried you forever.
No escape. Simple agony. Hell.
But, you came to life for me today.
This white cast. Your final moments of pain.
Did you have a small boy that loved you?
Did your Master feed you treats on warm summer days?
Did someone brush your fur through the seasons?
Your jaws are so large.
Your twisted image remains frozen in my mind.
I want to stroke the fur no longer seen.
I want to whisper in your ear, and tell you to hold on.
The Elysian Fields will be cool against your paws.

High Flight

Two hawks flew across my horizon last week.
Slender, smooth.
Sharp, acute turns.
Perfectly timed.
Soaring grace.
Together.

Peace

There is a peace in this space on the hill.
A quiet comfort that feels like the landscape and house have wrapped me in a big,
warm hug
Protecting me from the worries of the world outside.
I never thought I would find this.
I didn't think God listened anymore.
I was looking for peace through something or someone undefined.
And this place came to me.
Just when I was going to give up the search.
Perhaps angels do come in different packages.

Calm after the Storm

We were lucky.
The storm spared us
from power loss and ice dams.
This time.
Some were not so lucky.
They lost power, property, and some - their lives.
New England is a beautiful place.
Weather that can make each day a paradise
in Winter, Spring, Summer and Fall.
But weather patterns are changing.
The storms I welcomed in youth can now become threatening.
Violent.
The rain turns to floods.
The warm days to scorching fires.
Yes, patterns are changing.
But, there is the calm that follows the storm,
bringing the wonder of blue skies,
the radiance of sunshine
and the song of hope in the voices of the birds.
Storm. Calm. Hope.
The trifecta still works.

Extraordinary day

The early fall sun pours its rays across my back porch.
I'm reclining on the lounger, soaking in the beauty of this place. Birds, russet-colored mums, my cats golden fur against my feet.
Traffic noise echoes across neighborhood yards. Birds gently peep in the trees around the lawn. A beautiful symphony.

This moment is precious. It will never come again and I'm living the moments and sounds completely.

A hammer is making it's presence known now. Two dogs at the end of the street are arguing over their space. My cat's purr reminds me of his muted contentment on this most rare day of days.

The wind is quietly breezing through the leaves of the stately maples that stand watch over the yard, while the late-summer crickets chirp out their end-of-season statement from the grass below.

Thank you for the blue sky painted with spider-web clouds.
Thank you for the internal silence that coats my soul.
Thank you for the beauty of these moments on this very ordinary, extraordinary day.

Independence

Sitting.
Cross-legged.
On the floor.
My cushion after a magic carpet ride.
Haven't I been here once before?
Undressed rooms.
Undressed walls.
Empty halls.
Prepped for evolution.
A collage of memories paint the far reaches of my mind.
Vibrant hues.
But, I've finally come home.
To me.

Fall in New England

I'm driving through tree-lined back-roads painted under a canopy of golden and sienna leaves.
Draping all around my car.
Pops of cherry red.
Smudges of brown.
A sprinkle of green.
The music of Mozart on the airwaves.
A harvest of colors and sounds on an October New England morning.

I remember these days as a child.
Walking home from school and looking for the driest golden leaves I could step on, just to hear the crunch under foot.
Today was one of those days.
Blue sky.
Cooler temps.
A taste of winter in the air.
The golden leaves on the sides of the roadway waiting for a child's footstep, and the crunch to follow.
Timeless.

Midnight

In the still of the night,
under the warmth of the blankets,
his fingers find my hand.
He wraps them silently around my fingertips.
I hear him breathe.
Slowly.
Deeply.
He's fast asleep.
But, somehow, his love for me is there.
His gentle touch in slumber
fills my heart.
Love.
It never sleeps.

I give thanks

I give thanks to this world that I live in,
to the trees and the skies up above,
to the blue of the oceans and rivers,
to the mountains which echo His love.
Time speeds through decades and lifetimes,
and we all become caught in the craze.
But at the end of each day when I'm praying,
my silence still shouts out His praise.

Becoming

Becoming me.
A difficult discovering of lost memories, births, deaths, and forgotten dreams.
A painful process of taking risks, losing, winning, and waiting.
A tender time of holding friendships to the light,
touching the qualities and imperfections woven within,
and sometimes doing without.

Becoming me.
Learning to believe in a friend that has lived in my soul since time began.
To forgive the sins of the fathers, and of the self.
To test the limits of laughter, and tears.
To heed the call of instinct, and not question actions guided by love.

Becoming me.
Understanding the importance of my life.
Embracing pleasure. Looking out for me,
yet treating all spirits with the gentleness and independence I allot myself.

Becoming me.
Realizing that failure is another path to success,
That sorrow is not infinite,
That happiness is fragile,
and knowing that beyond today, there will never be
another me.

Printed in the United States
by Baker & Taylor Publisher Services